NYCTOPHILIA

Sonnets

Copyright © 2025 Zachary J. Horvitz All rights reserved.

No part of this book may be reproduced, or stored in a retrieval system, or transmitted in any form or by any means, electronic, mechanical, photocopying, recording, or otherwise, without the written permission of the author.

ISBN 978-1-7371519-4-4

NYCTOPHILIA

Sonnets

Zachary J. Horvitz

I

You take away all those whom you are not.
(Spectral nightling, mouth and cosmic tongue.)
You kill the final consort whom you wrought
To find me hollowed by the Second Sun,
Erase each person who once claimed to be
Incarnate life of that which only you
Behold in mirror-darkness, auto-see.
None who feign to know you must speak true,
And none whose reign is yours will you outlast.
At night I feel you syphoning my corpse,
O rightful necromancer for this task.
Defeat all those who replicate your course!
Dismember, Goddess, all that which can take form.
Dismember now my shape, through me reborn.

II

To walk inside the aeon of the Sabbath,
Where Sabbath is an aeon unto self,
Sleep is one such doorway of this habit,
Wherewith we take a stroll within our death.
We fall upon an endless bed of starlight,
We walk the fields of endless waking rest.
It's good to recognize that such a rite
Is open to each soul, without protest.
It's good to undisguise the face of life,
That likes to hide itself in serious jest.
Most perfect peace, behind the mask of strife —
Like sitting there, aloft the lunar crest,
In all those waking dreams of silver death
And radiant darkness, lived, not only dreamt.

III

The rhododendron garden gives me life —
Like being dead to all that does not flower.
The brainwound is a liquid darkness, rife
With tendrils, digging plasma — magic power.
I love to walk englobed by that domain,
At peace to think in iambs without thought.
I love to die into the next refrain
Of metered incarnations, fivefold lot,
And ever wormhole through the narrow place
Where hope of entry kills us: *Gehinnom*...
(Save for the sovereign, Entropy, our grace!)
Until I hang in Heaven with my mom.
The night's revolving doorway spits me out.
Nightmongers must be poor. (Nothing to tout.)

IV

Keep quiet for the sake of Heaven's court,
And hear these sentences while you remain —
This godsent life is comparable to sport,
In that the every outcome of the game
Matters naught, beyond the bounds of play.
All things be equal 'neath the starlit sky,
And all things = being, the yea or nay
Regardless unto us, who always die.
Oh, never flee the shadow that is death,
Lest you must run forever. No "before,"
No "everafter." One must be as deft
As sentinels whose stillness becomes lore.
The animate silence speaks the tongue of mimes
When future comes to be in present times.

V

The healing fire of heartbreak is the horse
That breaches every prison from within.
You ride the flames of war, an equine force
Inside the walls of spacetime, cosmic sin.
The horse is made of everlasting light,
And penetrates the shell of every Troy.
The cities that enclose the gods' delight,
And relegate to demons every joy,
Cannot be sieged by normal battlements.
They are besieged by secret, other means —
The heart's own solar system, elements
And starform syphoned into baths & streams,
Known to Apollo and to Parsifal —
Radiant heart-rays, Hyperion's arsenal.

VI

Because I did not come to conquer you,
And waited steady at the stronghold's gate,
A scribe to circumscripture's polar moods,
Ten years was as a single nightfall's fate.
I slept a woodland sleep for half those years,
A desiccated spirit in the dark.
I dreamt of sprouting flowers from the ears,
I dreamt my skin became a kind of bark.
Perhaps I traveled to the Nether-Time...
Perhaps you've also seen the realm of ghosts?
If I am "dead but dreaming" [Deicide]
That would explain why you love me the most:
Supernal love does not exist on earth.
A perfect afterlife — your heart, your hearth.

VII

Two crows are perched upon your shoulders now,
Of which perhaps I am the blackest one.
The other flies away without a how
To fly by day beneath eclipse of sun.
Morrígan, I know you — should I fear
What ageless power draws these birds to perch?
Morrígan, the epoch's end is here...
The fire in you must bring a second birth
Of self and world, the lovechildren of warlust.
Morrígan, I too dance 'round a pyre,
That threatens to incinerate my trust —
When battles break and I become the sire
Of kingdoms I have always called my own;
Of kingdoms I have longed for, yet to know.

VIII

Alone at night, barefoot across the cool
Stone pathway past the solemn sway of trees,
A little puppy breaks his master's rule
And comes to sit by one whom I call 'me.'
All that I'm told to be through others' eyes,
From inside-out feels only like a space
In which I take a tranquil swim — alive
To liquid darkness, astral-warm embrace.
I swim inside a dense infinity,
The comfort of a vast and peaceful womb.
The master does not know her dog perceives
That silent blessing hidden in the loom
Of stars, the thread and weave of endless light —
The thread and weave of endless onyx light.

IX

To make an offering of space and time,
One's self must be eternal sacrifice.
Restore the substance of this very mind,
And offer up the body and its life.
Make matter into magic once again.
Let burn the final embers of this fire.
Let fall the Hydra's many beastial heads
And leave them to a total cosmic pyre.
Through every kind of funeral and pain,
Through darkmost depths of void, to cleanse and bathe,
You saunter through a mushroomcloud, unscathed,
Emerging by re-birth, nor mad nor sane.
At last the opaque mirror's perfect glare
Sees you, beyond the foul and beyond fair.

X

To look upon the one who gazes back,
You must withstand this dark opacity:
A mirror-void beyond the color black,
Where every star returns to vacancy.
A dying Aztec warrior's final dream:
A darker stone than what John Dee once stole
(Amidst decaying eyes, the brightest gleam)
From his 'New World,' for prophecy and gold.
To know the deepest texture of that sphere,
To dive into that one obsidian mind,
(The mind of night that nullifies all fear)
You must consent to life and death entwined.
Behold now what can't be seen directly! —
Within the skull, the brain without a psyche.

XI

My single compass is the midnight sun,
A star above the passing mortal world,
From which all sonnets have in time begun,
The sound of light that often goes unheard —
Until the one who listens is no more
And only song remains throughout the whole
Expanse of space, forever and before
You think of how to reach a timeless goal.
I am what that sound has always been,
A darkness that is bright beyond compare —
A diamond lamp, that does not shine for him
In whom the dark and light are not a pair.
As this world dies, I sift through sediment
Of astral life, celestial ornament.

XII

I can't invoke you through poetic song.
Nor spell nor rhyme will conjure blessing here.
The cunning pact that Faustus made was wrong...
Love is not love, which falters when it fears
The freedom of another's willful heart.
A knight of faith in Denmark took the leap
Of resignation, infinite: the start
Of something one might call eternal sleep,
But rather I might term his waking life
At last allowed to live itself to death.
I can't invoke the powers of the night,
Mephisto nor the petty magic left,
To help you trust what I can feel is felt.
Please help me see what you want for yourself.

XIII

I stored a precious vase within my chest,
That held a precious item: empty space.
The formless jewel, enclosed inside a nest
Of glassy barriers, melted to the taste
Of amaranthine quartz, hibiscus rain.
I drank the stone to death, by which I mean
The liquid substance stoned me. Bliss and pain —
This diamond heart, a molten crystal dream
Whose destiny was made to alter phase,
To change into another form of matter:
A plasma pooled beyond the winter haze,
Into the night-washed sky, a dark hereafter.
The deepest human cave does house a treasure;
Beneath this cave of bone, space without measure.

XIV

The tithes of winter keep me winterbound.
(Snowfall on the mountains, almost May.)
I go to thank Chief Niwot's burial mound
Before release from half a decade's stay.
I go to supplicate those frozen hills
With twilight hymns, small gifts to strew the trails;
A euphony of darkness, shouts and shrills.
(To square the circle, circle magic squares.)
Oh offer me thine own ubiquity,
Beyond all death and every present doubt.
I offer back my form and finity
To life once more untethered, Gracious Mount!
Beneath the care and auspice of thy shade,
The winter dues have now been rightly paid.

XV

Intoxication by the smallest things,
Entrancement by the most common events...
Thimbles, teacups; a set of silver rings.
The winter snow. These late-falling sunsets.
Here, poised to die, without a dint of hope
(And to be born with neither cry nor fuss),
No Heaven's choir, and no angelic trope —
New realms and times must merit perfect trust.
For life is not a single lightning flash,
But boundless fire contained in tiny bulbs,
Whose blackened vestiges are God's own ash.
When finite spheres do shatter, unbound globes
Without circumference swallow every name
We give to אור אין סוף, the blackest flame.

XVI

I dive unto perpetual depths of dream,
Where uncaused apparitions lodge themselves;
A geodomic strobelight on the scene,
Rainbow-bodies from four quarters, radiant elves;
Sonic waves from extrasensory realms;
A horde of nondead armies, paramortal;
The superswarm of orgiastic whelms;
A moshpit of celestial forms, toroidal,
And sifted through an hourglassy hole —
A selenite gyration, serpent-dance;
A vast transparent column, lighted pole,
Unwielded, oft-concealèd... *necromance.*
O nightborne daemon, you, deathbound to life!
— Thy wakeful sleep, abundant with all life.

XVII

No word can be more infinite than none,
No phrase can speak superior than the day
We first saw Nova Scotia, under sun
That bent through fog, inviting us to play.
No chance to get to zero from a step
Into numeric seeking for some thing.
Recall Church Point, where rock and seaweed swept
Acadian shores; the wind itself was tinged
With happy moods, that meant more than we could
Each other mean; the weather would outlast
What was not anything but kelp and wood.
No day is more than that; all speech is crass
Attempt to be what is not one nor two,
But infinitely neither: void and you.

XVIII

The canvas is a crystal made of mind,
The canvas is a crystal made of light.
All wavelengths and each vessel, space and time.
All blankness and each brushstroke — both are right.
Compound the spectral colors of the spheres,
Compound the astral music one might hear
On other worlds and given other times,
Beyond this reach and register of rhyme.
One holds as real whatever happenstance
Occurrence is, so why should one neglect
The wane and wax of synchronous events?
For such a magic show one turns askance...
Yet you are guide to all who would believe;
You guide us, *watch the soundscape crystals weave.*

XIX

Advance the help of hidden embers' heat,
A dance of black and red upon the mound.
By lighted coals uncovered we shall meet,
And sing the song of toads, a strange green sound.
Advance the steps of little members' feet,
All creatures whom we cannot hope perceive.
Within a wood where what we sow, we reap,
Awake! — to what one cannot yet conceive.
Advance good tidings as the moon is full,
Or bloodshot with a different colored blood:
The bluest tint become the lunar pull,
Like veins outpouring azurite, a flood
Of teal, instead of crimson waters, where
Upon the lunar face — a liquid glare.

XX

While making way to the depth of the heart —
A wellspring, where one can find no fathom,
Where nothing comes and nothing can depart,
Confused wayfarers seeking something gathered.
Astrologers and other kinds of guides
Gave their best wisdom for an ample price.
Assuming costumes, under a gnostic guise,
A mystic fairground did sometime arise.
Whole mirrored hallways and houses of fun
Accumulated on the camping site.
Some took drugs that sent them to the Sun,
Some saw angelic bugs, made of pure light.
But all this seemed like fancy circus stuff.
Naught was there, no heart, mere magic dust.

XXI

As one would sit upon a regal chair,
You are afloat upon the globe of earth,
A universal monarch of affairs,
No thought of gain nor loss, nor death nor birth.
A looking-bloom: the forehead's treasure trove;
A portal to prismatic colored worlds,
Where sound and light are made of lucid love,
And insubstantial speech like smoke unfurls.
Speak dead tongues to all those happy beings
Who wake from slumber with your helpful chants—
Which make the seamless be just as it seems,
Among the rising birds and trees and plants.
A huge procession 'round your primal seat —
All things at once abound about your feet.

XXII

Once before Queen Mab had been with him.
The sovereign faerie's heart was sometime tied
To that young soldier's all too garrulous mind.
Only the gleam of amethyst in her eyes,
That gentle violet light, could keep him quiet.
What did Romeo know of such a spell?
How many ballroom kisses could compare?
All sprites return to air, at last abscond
Their crystal gaze, combusting many fates.
Mercutio didn't need the king of cats,
Good Tybalt, to entice a public duel.
And Romeo didn't need to come between.
The consequence was hanging in the stars
When Mab departed from Mercutio's dreams.

XXIII

The seeds of time bear ever timely swathes.
Thus to regret the circumambulation
Of stars (thy solar legs upon time's lathe)
Is to ignore the mouth of fabulation —
Ecstatic, eating time, the food of space.
Reanimating spiral destinies,
This floodborne light, of liquid metal, taste!
(A prison shell, congealèd entropies...)
Hah hah, hah hah. I love the sheen of night.
I die into the everlasting shroud
That is my life... dark fabric for a sprite.
Devoid of all but Void, *Ab Plenum, Ad!*
For you this realm is monstrous, to avoid;
For us, voidwalkers — fortress, home, and joy.

XXIV

I swallow lightning bolts of molten lead
That erelong drowned me deep within the dark
Electric watercourse, where I am fed
Unto the *nagas, thelim...* serpent-sparks.
I see a sovereign king emerge from haze
Gone skyward past the harrowing, dormant gods
That sleep inside volcanoes, mountain caves,
And offer human beings celestial laws
Whenever soul and starlight from us fade
As common view, and other forces thrall
The highest good beneath nefarious shade.
Let not temporal measure make a stall;
Let deities digest their own dark matter,
Even if my name be on the platter.

XXV

I am a withering tree amid the garden.
I am the seed that dies into the field.
I am the death of time, I am time's warden.
I speak because I love this moment's yield.
Here with me, and also here as absence.
Absence is the kiss of waking rest.
I cannot kiss you, so I save my breath;
I cannot kiss you, so my speaking lapses...
Yes! there is ever time to know time's end.
Yes! one can offer patience to perfection.
Perfection is the formless, absent-friend,
Whose friendship is itself mine own redemption.
Once upon night's calm and careful auspice,
I felt within my core her luminous darkness...

www.ingramcontent.com/pod-product-compliance
Lightning Source LLC
Chambersburg PA
CBHW060413080526
44583CB00012B/560